Dual Diagnosis
Drug Addiction
and Mental Illness

ILLICIT AND MISUSED DRUGS

ILLICIT AND MISUSED DRUGS

Dual Diagnosis
Drug Addiction
and Mental Illness

by Malinda Miller

Mason Crest

Mason Crest
370 Reed Road
Broomall, Pennsylvania 19008
www.masoncrest.com

Printed in the Hashemite Kingdom of Jordan.

First printing
9 8 7 6 5 4 3 2 1

Library of Congress Cataloging-in-Publication Data

Miller, Malinda, 1979-
Dual diagnosis : drug addiction and mental illness / Malinda Miller.
    p. cm.
ISBN 978-1-4222-2430-4 (hardcover)
ISBN 978-1-4222-2424-3 (hardcover series)
ISBN 978-1-4222-9294-0 (ebook)
1. Drug addicts—Mental health. 2. Mentally ill—Substance use.
3. Dual diagnosis—Patients—Rehabilitation. I. Title.
RC564.M537 2013
616.86—dc23
                                    2012013832

Interior design by Benjamin Stewart.
Cover design by Torque Advertising + Design.
Produced by Harding House Publishing Services, Inc.
www.hardinghousepages.com

This book is meant to educate and should not be used as an alternative to appropriate medical care. Its creators have made every effort to ensure that the information presented is accurate—but it is not intended to substitute for the help and services of trained professionals.

 # CONTENTS

INTRODUCTION

Addicting drugs are among the greatest challenges to health, well-being, and the sense of independence and freedom for which we all strive—and yet these drugs are present in the everyday lives of most people. Almost every home has alcohol or tobacco waiting to be used, and has medicine cabinets stocked with possibly outdated but still potentially deadly drugs. Almost everyone has a friend or loved one with an addiction-related problem. Almost everyone seems to have a solution neatly summarized by word or phrase: medicalization, legalization, criminalization, war-on-drugs.

For better and for worse, drug information seems to be everywhere, but what information sources can you trust? How do you separate misinformation (whether deliberate or born of ignorance and prejudice) from the facts? Are prescription drugs safer than "street" drugs? Is occasional drug use really harmful? Is cigarette smoking more addictive than heroin? Is marijuana safer than alcohol? Are the harms caused by drug use limited to the users? Can some people become addicted following just a few exposures? Is treatment or counseling just for those with serious addiction problems?

These are just a few of the many questions addressed in this series. It is an empowering series because it provides the information and perspectives that can help people come to their own opinions and find answers to the challenges posed by drugs in their own lives. The series also provides further resources for information and assistance, recognizing that no single source has all the answers. It should be of interest and relevance to areas of study spanning biology, chemistry, history, health, social studies and more. Its efforts to provide a real-world context for the information that is clearly presented but not overly simplified should be appreciated by students, teachers, and parents.

The series is especially commendable in that it does not pretend to pose easy answers or imply that all decisions can be made on the basis of simple facts: some challenges have no immediate or simple solutions, and some solutions will need to rely as much upon basic values as basic facts. Despite this, the series should help to at least provide a foundation of knowledge. In the end, it may help as much by pointing out where the solutions are not simple, obvious, or known to work. In fact, at many points, the reader is challenged to think for him- or herself by being asked what his or her opinion is.

A core concept of the series is to recognize that we will never have all the facts, and many of the decisions will never be easy. Hopefully, however, armed with information, perspective, and resources, readers will be better prepared for taking on the challenges posed by addictive drugs in everyday life.

— Jack E. Henningfield, Ph.D.

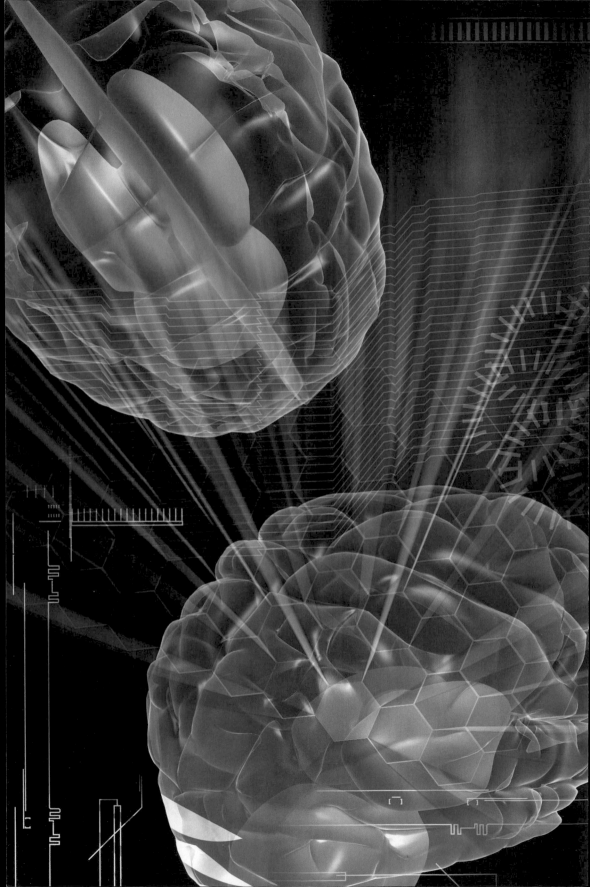

7 This Is Your Brain

Imagine that your brain is a giant communications center, the hub of all your body's communication needs. In order for your body to function, the brain must communicate with itself and with every other part of your body. According to researchers who have studied this three-pound communications center, *billions* of messages are sent and received throughout the brain in a single day, using a complex network of nerve cells (which are called neurons).

Neurons are made up of three structures: dendrites (several branch-like limbs protruding from the cell body, which receive information), the cell body (the neuron's central part, which examines information), and an axon (a single cable-like tail, which sends information). The

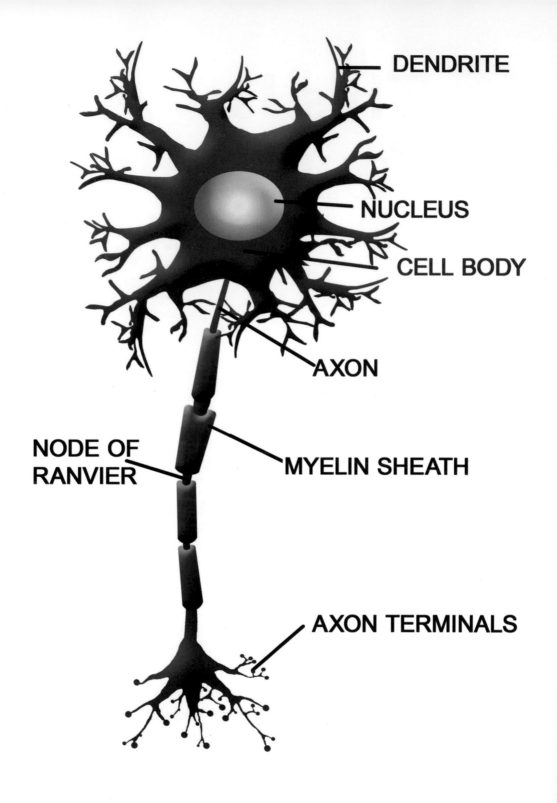

DENDRITE

NUCLEUS

CELL BODY

AXON

NODE OF
RANVIER

MYELIN SHEATH

AXON TERMINALS

end of the axon contains several terminal buttons, which overlap the dendrites of other neurons. The neurons, however, don't actually touch each other; they leave a space between called the synapse.

Communication Between Brain Cells

Because neurons don't actually touch each other, they must use special chemicals called neurotransmitters to send and receive messages. This sending and receiving can be a complicated process.

Imagine that you're an outfielder in a baseball game and you want to send a message to the catcher. You attach a note to the ball in your hand, wind up, swing your arm, release the ball, and throw it toward home plate. The baseball, with message attached, flies through air, across mid-field, right to the catcher's glove. Though your center fielder's glove never touched the catcher's glove, you were able to get the message to him. How? You used the ball.

Neurons work together in a similar way in the brain. Using our baseball analogy, you, the center fielder, would be the sending nerve cell, called the presynaptic neuron. The message you want to send is the note attached to the baseball. The catcher would be the receiving cell, called the postsynaptic neuron. To get the message from you, the center fielder (presynaptic neuron), to the catcher (postsynaptic neuron), you have to throw the ball. In the brain, instead of using a baseball to carry the message, the presynaptic neuron (the sending nerve cell) sends its message using chemical neurotransmitters. To throw the ball, the neuron "fires," releasing the neurotransmitters (the baseball) into the synapse (the space between the nerve cells or the space between centerfield and home) to carry its message.

Once released into the synapse, the neurotransmitter (the ball) looks for the postsynaptic neuron's (receiving cell's or catcher's) receptors (catcher's glove). When the presynaptic neuron's neurotransmitters bind with the postsynaptic neuron's receptors (when the ball finds its way to the glove), the message is delivered.

Once the message is delivered (once the catcher takes your note off the ball), the receiving cell (the catcher) doesn't need the neurotransmitter anymore (the ball), so it releases the neurotransmitters back into the synapse (throws the ball, without its message, back into the air between home and centerfield). These used neurotransmitters will remain in the synapse (the ball will stay between the home and the centerfield) until the original sending cell (the center fielder) takes them back (center fielder catches or picks up the ball). This process of taking neurotransmitters back again is called reuptake.

Now imagine that you want to send a billion messages to the catcher. You'd need quite a few baseballs to send those messages! Scientists estimate the brain uses more than a million neurons to send messages over a quadrillion synapses.

Problems in Brain Communication

Communication in the brain is a complicated process made up of several steps, any of which can run into problems:

- The presynaptic neuron doesn't fire correctly (center fielder has a poor arm).
- The brain doesn't produce enough neurotransmitters (there aren't enough balls to carry the messages).

The space between neurons is called the synapse. Neurotransmitters carry the messages across this space.

Dual Diagnosis—Drug Addiction and Mental Illness 13

- The postsynaptic neuron has too few receptors (catcher doesn't catch well or doesn't have a glove).
- The postsynaptic neuron's receptors get blocked (a base runner blocks the catcher's glove, keeping the catcher from catching the ball).
- Enzymes (other brain chemicals) destroy too much of the neurotransmitters remaining in the synapse (fans steal the balls before they're caught).
- Too much or too little neurotransmitter is taken back by the sending cell (the center fielder hogs the used ball or drops the ball when it's returned).

Any disruption of the communication process between neurons can result in psychological disorders—what most of us call mental illness.

Many psychological disorders result primarily from problems with neurotransmitters (how they are released, how much neurotransmitter is present, how much is taken back by the sending cell). To date, scientists have identified over twenty kinds of neurotransmitters in the brain, with each being used in multiple parts of the brain. They have also found links between certain neurotransmitters and specific psychological conditions. Depression and bipolar disorder, for example, are both linked to the neurotransmitters serotonin, norepinephrine, and dopamine.

Neurotransmitters also play important roles in how drugs affect our bodies.

Some of the Parts of the Brain

The cerebrum: the largest and most important part of the brain that controls higher thoughts and reasoning, memory, voluntary movement, sensory perception (sight, sound, touch, etc.), speech, language, learning, and perception. The cerebrum is made up of four lobes, each controlling its own area of function: the frontal lobe, the parietal lobe, the occipital lobe, and the temporal lobe.

The cerebellum: the part of the brain located beneath the cerebrum at the back of the head that controls automatic, involuntary posture, balance, and muscular coordination.

The brain stem: the brain section below the cerebrum and in front of the cerebellum through which all body signals must pass to move from the spinal cord to the brain. This part of the brain controls reflexes and involuntary actions.

The limbic system: a group of structures that create a person's emotional make-up, including pleasure and aggression.

The hypothalamus: a part of the limbic system that balances overall body metabolism and regulates body temperature, emotions, hunger, thirst, and sleep patterns.

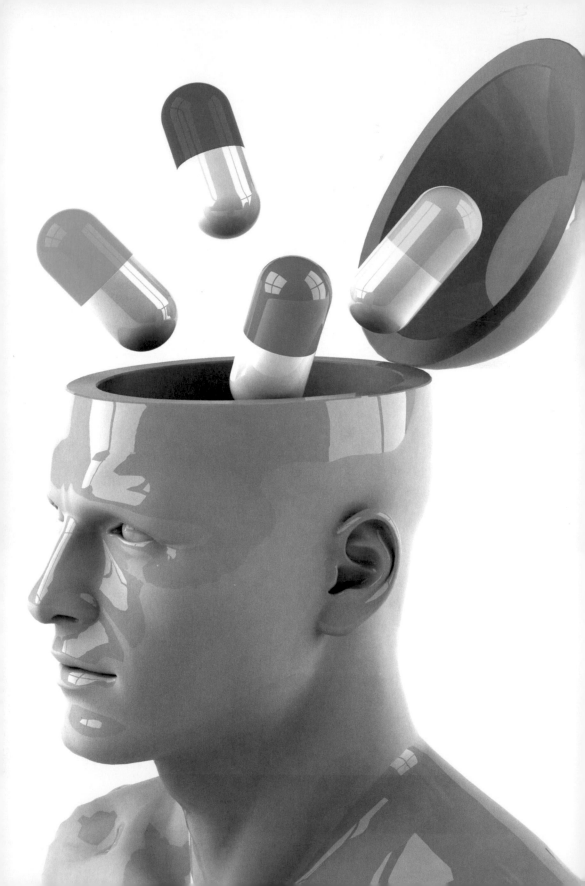

2 This Is Your Brain on Drugs

Did you ever see the anti-drug ad that showed an egg and said, "This is your brain"? Then it showed the egg being cracked and fried, while the voiceover said, "This is your brain on drugs. Get the picture?"

It's not actually quite that simple of course. Drugs can have beneficial effects as well as negative. But good or bad, they're powerful chemicals that can change the way our brains behave.

A brain is like a complicated machine.

What's a Drug?

According to the scientific community, a drug is a chemical substance that affects how the body works; when not abused, it is useful in the diagnosis, treatment, or prevention of a disease or as a component of a medication.

When chemicals enter your body, they can interfere with the neurotranmitters'
ability to carry messages across the gaps between neurons.

Chapter 2—This Is Your Brain on Drugs

It's filled with cells and chemicals that are engaged in countless and constant interactions. Your brain runs your entire body. It makes sure that you keep breathing and that your heart keeps pumping. It tells you to eat when you are hungry and to go to sleep when you're tired. Your brain decides whom you like and who to avoid, when to watch television and when to read a book, if you want to play baseball or if you'd rather go out for track.

The brain and the body are in constant communication through the neurotransmitters we discussed in the last chapter. Drugs are chemicals that often interact or interfere with the mechanisms your brain uses to send information from one cell to another. This can be beneficial to the entire body—but it can also be harmful in some cases. Imagine that your brain is like a computer that's running all the assembly lines in a factory. If you poured a glass of water onto the computer, you would short-circuit the assemblage of wires, transmitters, and connections. Drugs can short-circuit your brain in a similar way.

Powerful Chemicals

Look at the list below. Can you tell what these items have in common?

aerosol deodorant
PAM® cooking spray
chewing tobacco
White-Out®
marijuana
nail polish remover
spot cleaner
steroids

Coricidin HBP (cough and cold medicine)
Ritalin
beer
permanent markers
gasoline
rubber cement
hair spray
morphine
Tylenol® with Codeine
Oxycontin
cocaine
LSD
spray paint

Can you guess? First here's what they *don't* have in common: they are not all illegal; they are not all medicines; they are not all solids; they are not all liquids; they are not all gasses or aerosols; they cannot all be purchased at local stores; they are not all legally available; and they are not all "bad."

So what do they have in common?

They are all chemical substances.

They can all be used to get "high."

They all have the potential to be addictive.

Every item on the preceding list, if inhaled, ingested, or injected, has the potential to produce a physical effect in the body. That effect can be good or bad, healthy or unhealthy—depending on use. That is the nature of chemicals. Hair spray, for example, can have the positive effect of taming unruly hair when applied appropriately; but when inhaled repeatedly it can cause heart failure or suffocation. The cough and cold medicine called Coricidin HBP when taken as instructed can ease the runny nose, sneezing, and cough of the common cold; but when

These ordinary household products don't look like drugs—but they can all be used to get high.

taken in very high doses can cause **hallucinations**, *seizures*, brain injury, and death.

Some of these chemicals have legitimate uses that were never intended to include anything relating to the body: spot removers are chemicals designed to break down the compositions of tough-to-remove stains; gasoline is a chemical designed to be highly combustible to produce power for combustion engines; rubber cement is a chemical designed to be used as an adhesive. Each has a positive, productive function when used as intended; but if used as a means to get high, these can chemically alter the brain.

In that sense, every item on the list could be considered a "drug"; in other words, it is a chemical that produces a physical effect by changing the way the mind or body works.

How Do Drugs Work?

Jerome takes a slow deep drag on a joint. He takes another, then another. Slowly he begins to feel relaxed and spacey; then he gets hungry. He's experiencing "the munchies."

Natalie looks at the yellow smiley-faced pill in her hand and, at the urging of her friends, pops it into her mouth and washes it down with a big gulp of bottled water. Thirty minutes later she's convulsing on the floor.

Mark jams a needle of anabolic steroids into his thigh once a week to bulk up his muscles and increase his strength. In just a matter of weeks, his moods begin swinging between depression and rage and his face erupts in acne.

What's happening to these kids? Each one is ingesting a chemical: one is inhaled, one is swallowed, and one is

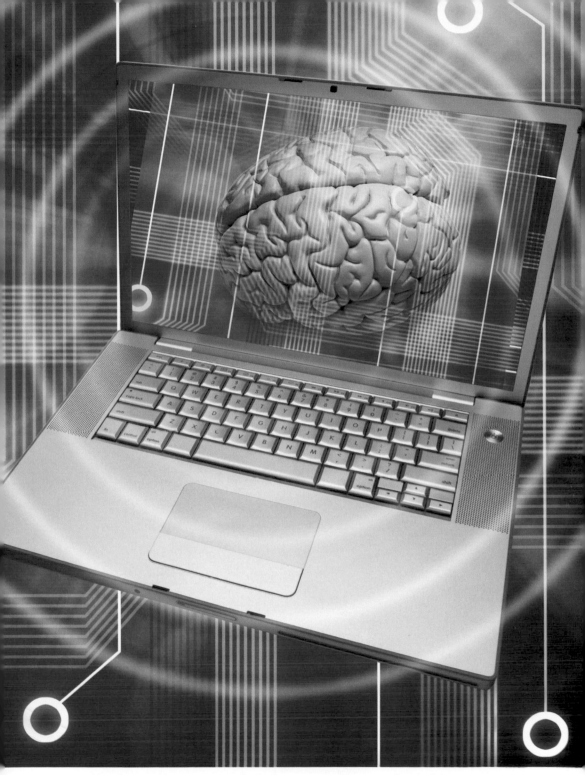

Your brain is like a computer. And when you put dangerous chemicals into your brain, it's a little like pouring water onto your keyboard!

Dual Diagnosis—Drug Addiction and Mental Illness 23

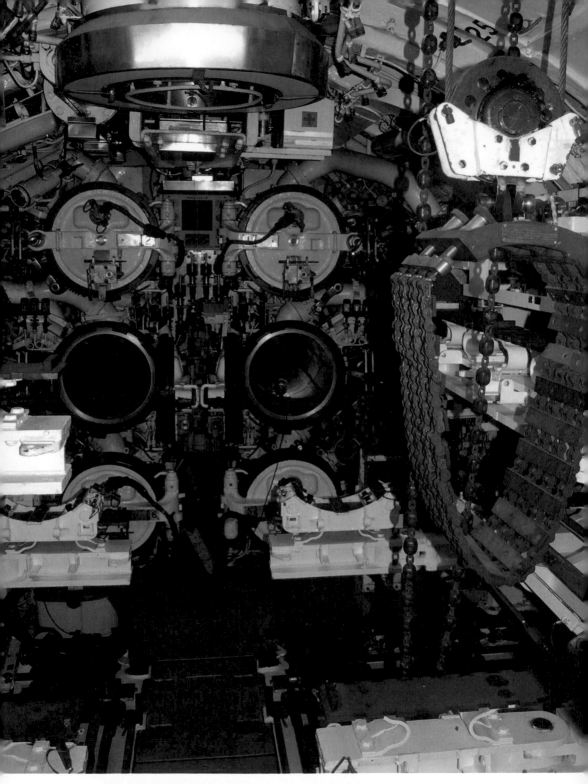

The control room of a submarine is a complicated place—and so is your brain!

injected. All three are experiencing those chemicals' effects on their brains and body—each chemical causing a different set of effects.

To understand how drugs affect the body and why different drugs do different things we have to first look at the brain and how it functions. We've already talked about the brain as a baseball game and as a computer. Now we'll use another metaphor.

Imagine you are the captain of a nuclear submarine. In order to operate your submarine effectively you have to man the control room where you receive information from command team members stationed at instrument panels in the control room with you and from other controllers in distant parts of the sub (for example, the engine room, the rudder control room, the sonar room, the torpedo room, the maneuver room, the mess hall, the cabins, the store room). You and your team members have to continuously monitor, process, and react to any information provided; you have to communicate with each other and with other parts of the sub. As long as communication is clear and unhindered, you can operate the sub safely; but when signals are distorted or transmissions clouded, you run the risk of serious damage to the sub and personal injury or harm to yourself or your crew.

Your brain is like the control room of a submarine. It's the command center of your body—not just your thought processes, but your bodily functions as well. The brain regulates your body temperature; it identifies sources of pain; it coordinates the movements of your arms and legs so you can walk, run, hit a ball, or clap your hands; it orchestrates your air flow and larynx so that you can talk, hum, or sing; it makes sense of visual images; it interprets sounds; it allows you to imagine and dream. To make these things happen, the brain processes information and communicates that information within itself and the rest of the body.

Communication in a submarine happens when voice or data signals travel over wires or wireless frequencies from the sender to the receiver. As the captain, you send a message by speaking into a microphone, which carries your voice electronically over communication wires to the person with whom you wish to communicate. In the brain, instead of using wires or frequencies, messages are carried by nearly 100 billion brain cells—neurons. Communication happens when electrical impulses travel through the neurons in the process we described back in chapter 1. This kind of communication between neurons is carried out literally billions of times per second to accomplish your bodily functions and thought processes, including everything from blowing your nose, to sleeping, to breathing, to reading a book, to having sexual impulses.

For our minds and bodies to work properly, however, communication between brain cells must stay in good working order. Inhaled or ingested chemical substances alter brain chemistry, especially the neurotransmitters (how much the sending neuron releases to carry the signal, how much is accepted by the receiving neuron, and how much stays in the synapse), and when brain chemistry is altered, neuron communication is disrupted or breaks down. And when communication between neurons breaks down, a person's thinking, feelings, and physical abilities change.

Substance Abuse and Behavior

Most of us have seen someone who has had too much to drink, and these people share some typical behaviors:

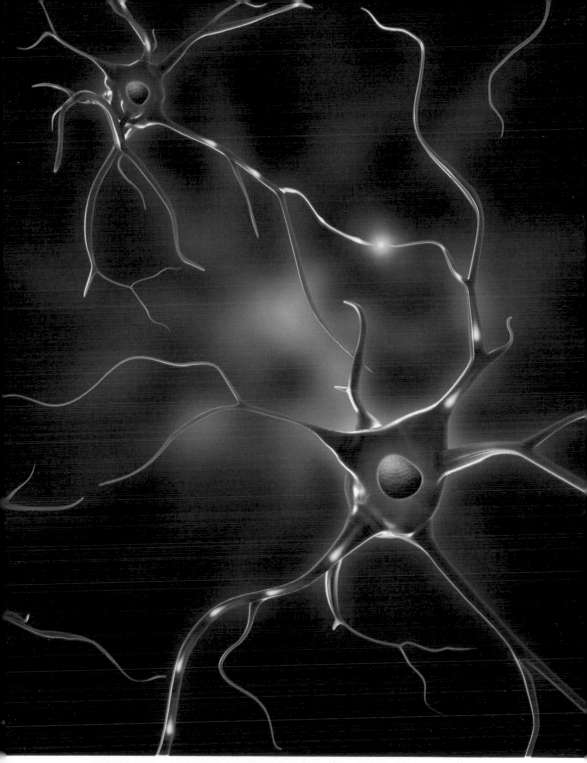

Messages are constantly being passed between the neurons in your body. When chemicals interfere with this process, the way your brain and mind behaves will be changed.

Types of Neurotransmitters in the Brain

Neurotransmitters are the chemical messengers that carry electrical impulses from one brain cell, across the synapse (the space in between cells) to another nerve cell. Different types of messages require different types of neurotransmitters. These are just a few:

Serotonin
Dopamine
GABA (Gamma-aminobutyric acid)
Glycine
Acetylcholine
Epinephrine
Norepinephrine

Substance abuse can alter how much of these chemical messengers are produced, how they carry their messages, and whether or not they are able to deliver the message to the next cell. Different drug substances may affect different neurotransmitters, but all are necessary for the brain's proper functioning.

their speech may become slurred; they may fall down a lot; they may look hot or flushed; they may have difficulty walking or writing; they act stupid or say stupid things; they may become intensely emotional (angry, giddy, or sad); they may throw-up; they may get sleepy or pass out. All of these behaviors are rooted in alcohol's effect on the neurotransmitters in the brain, especially a single type of neurotransmitter called GABA.

Alcohol, however, doesn't disrupt the GABA neurotransmitters of every part of the brain at the same time or rate, which is why you see a progression of various symptoms in a drunken person over time. To understand how alcohol and other chemical substances affect those

A neurotransmitter acts like a bridge between nerve cells.

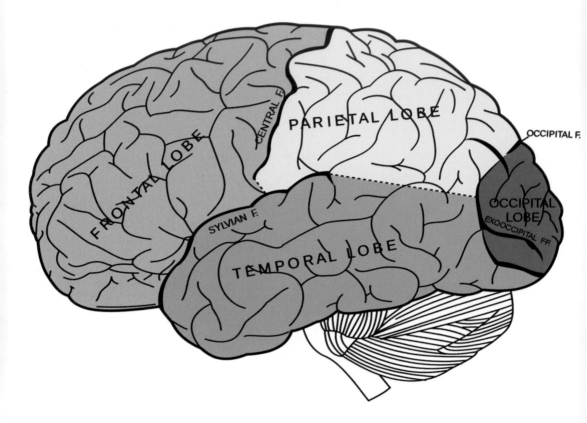

Different parts of your brain control different things that you do.

who use them, we need to understand how different parts of the brain control different aspects of our bodies, minds, and emotions.

So How Does a Drug Move Through the Brain?

Chemical substances don't affect the same parts of the brain in the same way at the same time.

Let's say that a person drinks a shot of whiskey or downs a pint of beer. The beverage moves down the throat, into the stomach, and into the intestines where the bulk of the beverage's alcohol content is absorbed into the bloodstream (about 20 percent is absorbed into the blood while passing through the stomach; the rest is absorbed through the small intestine). The blood then carries the alcohol throughout the body (liver, kidneys, brain, etc.).

When alcohol reaches the brain, it affects the cerebrum first. Since the cerebrum regulates thinking, self-control, and the ability to process sight, sound, smell, and other senses, the individual might first become more carefree, less reserved, and more talkative. She may have difficulty seeing or hearing well, and may not notice minor bumps, scrapes, and bruises since she isn't processing pain senses effectively. This person's ability to make good decisions, think clearly, or practice self-control may be impaired. All this happens when alcohol reaches this first part of the brain.

Then the alcohol moves from the cerebrum into the limbic system. Since this set of structures controls emotional responses and memory, the individual may become angry or overwhelmingly sad. She may cry and get into arguments. She might even throw things or become aggressive. And she might not remember her behavior the next morning.

Some scientists call the limbic system the place of "reward." Why? Because whenever we experience pleasurable circumstances, the limbic system releases a specific kind of neurotransmitter called "dopamine," which creates pleasurable feelings. The more dopamine released, the more pleasure we feel. Most abused chemical substances affect the limbic system, creating short-lasting feelings of pleasure called a "high."

From the limbic system the alcohol moves into the cerebellum, which controls and coordinates muscle movements and balance. Our intoxicated individual may become unsteady on her feet, lose her balance, or demonstrate stiff, jerky movements. This impact on the cerebellum is what police officers test for when they ask a suspected drunk driver to walk a straight line heel-to-toe or to touch his finger to his nose.

The alcohol continues its journey through the brain by next stopping at the hypothalamus (and the closely related pituitary gland, which controls hormone secretion). At this level of intoxication, the person may become sleepy, hungry, may need to urinate more, and may find her sexual desire has increased—although her ability to perform sexually is decreased.

Finally the alcohol arrives at the brain stem, which controls all the survival functions the body performs. These are things you are usually unaware of and have little conscious control over: breathing, body temperature regulation, heart rate, consciousness. A person with enough alcohol in her blood to impact brain-stem function can stop breathing, experience uncontrolled high blood pressure, or develop an out-of-control rise in body temperature, all of which can be fatal.

Not Just the Brain

The chemicals affect not only the brain but other parts of the body, too. How the drug is taken into the body impacts which additional parts of the body are affected.

Smoking, snorting, or inhaling will obviously irritate the nose, sinuses, airway, and lungs. Smokers develop coughs and get lung, mouth, and throat cancers. People who snort cocaine experience perpetual runny noses and chronic nosebleeds.

Substances that are ingested by swallowing, drinking, or eating (pills, liquids, laced food) irritate the linings of the stomach and intestines, can cause ulcers, can increase blood flow to the stomach, which reduces blood flow to other parts of the body.

Virtually all chemical substances enter the bloodstream, not just those injected, so all are processed through the circulatory system (heart, lungs, veins, arteries, kidneys, etc.) and pass through the body's most vital organs (including the pancreas and liver). This distribution throughout the vital organs explains liver disease in alcoholics and kidney failure in junkies.

Substance-Related Disorders

As human beings, our survival is dependent on eating, drinking, and breathing in order to maintain a healthy body. There are certain classes of substances, however, that interfere with our brain chemistry, bodily functions, and behavior when we eat, drink, smoke, breathe, or inject them. When a person becomes dependent on one of these drugs or medications, the medical world describes their condition as a substance-related disorder. When an individual has this type of disorder, he continues to use the substance even though significant behavior or health problems occur as a result of that use.

A substance-related disorder is characterized by serious and continued negative consequences to habitual use of an addictive substance over a twelve-month period.

In the 18th century, people already knew that alcohol could be dangerous. But just as today, alcohol production was a big part of society and the economy. Although alcohol is very addictive, it has remained legal in the United States (wih the exception of a short period during the early 20th century).

For example, Tom began to miss school in order to spend more time drinking. His use of alcohol made him physically ill, caused great distress to his parents, and resulted in many family arguments. Yet he continued to drink despite these problems.

Substances with the potential to cause addiction can affect the body physically and mentally. There are so many of these substances that they can be divided into eleven different categories. Some of these chemicals are legal and easily available, while others require a prescription from a physician. Still others are illegal under any circumstances because of their dangerous and potentially *lethal* qualities. Some of the substances act as *stimulants* to the brain and others act as *sedatives* or *depressants*.

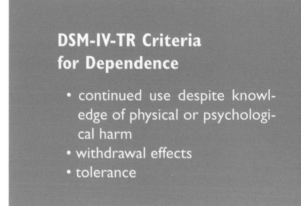

DSM-IV-TR Criteria for Dependence

- continued use despite knowledge of physical or psychological harm
- withdrawal effects
- tolerance

With the exception of caffeine, all of these eleven classes of substances have the potential to cause serious substance dependence (some of the common street names for these substances or variations of their chemicals appear in quotation marks).

- Alcohol: a depressant.
- Amphetamine, Dextroamphetamine, Methamphetamine ("speed," "crystal meth"): These are serious stimulants. This category also includes substances with *amphetamine*-like action such as certain *appetite suppressants*.

Drug Classifications

Drugs, both illicit and prescribed, fall into certain classifications depending on how they are used or how they affect the body.

- Stimulants speed up the body and the brain, increasing energy and alertness. Stimulants include ecstasy, amphetamines, caffeine, nicotine, and cocaine.

- Depressants slow down the body's normal activity by relaxing muscles and lowering brain activity. Opioids, alcohol, barbiturates, tranquilizers, and benzodiazepines are all depressants, or "downers."

- Hallucinogens, also known as psychedelics, are mood-altering drugs that affect the brain, and make the user see, feel, or hear things that are not really there. Hallucinogens include LSD and PCP. Ecstasy can also act as a hallucinogen.

- Marijuana, the most commonly used illicit drug, causes a variety of psychoactive effects so that it does not fit neatly into one drug category.

- Inhalants are drugs that are breathed in through the mouth or nose in gaseous form. They include many common household items such as gasoline, glue, and lighter fluid, among others.

- Antipsychotics are prescription drugs given to people who have mental conditions that cause delusions or hallucinations. Conditions commonly treated with antipsychotic medications include schizophrenia, bipolar disorder, delusional disorder, and psychotic depression.

- Antidepressants are prescribed for people coping with depression. There are a number of different varieties of antidepressants, including selective serotonin reuptake inhibitors (SSRIs) and monoamine oxidase inhibitors (MAOIs).

- Caffeine: This substance, which is found in coffee, black tea, cocoa, some soft drinks, and many prescription and **over-the-counter drugs**, is considered to be a minor stimulant.
- Cannabis (marijuana, "pot," "grass," "reefer"): the **psychoactive** ingredient in cannabis is tetra-hydro-cannabinol.
- Cocaine ("crack," "rock," "blow"): This is an **alkaloid** derived from coca leaves.
- Hallucinogens (psychedelic drugs): This diverse category includes ergot and related compounds such as lysergic acid diethylamide ("LSD," "acid"), phenyl-alkylamines (mescaline, "STP"), methylene dioxy-methamphetamine (MDMA, "ecstasy," "X"), indole alkaloids psilocybin ("shrooms"), dimethyltryptamine ("DMT"), and other substances. Psychedelic drugs like LSD and mescaline can have serious and long-lasting effects on the body. Some individuals may experience depression, **paranoia**, and frightening illusions while using psychedelics on one occasion and then have an opposite experience, including a general feeling of **euphoria**, the next time. Psychedelics work by affecting serotonin, one of the neurotransmitters in the brain.
- Inhalants: Substances such as glue, gasoline, and nitrous oxide are included in this category. Possibly because of easy accessibility of the substances and lack of education on the part of the users, inhalants are most often used by younger people. Inhalants are among the most dangerous substances of abuse as they can kill instantly. Individuals who do survive can suffer permanent damage because brain cells are destroyed by the use of inhalants. Headaches and stomach discomfort are the usual results of use.

- Nicotine: The addictive ingredient in cigarettes.
- Opioids: Morphine, heroin ("smack"), codeine, hydromorphone, methadone, opium, percodan, oxycodone, meperidine, fentanyl, and medications such as pentazocine and buprenorphine are included in this classification.
- Sedatives, *hypnotics*, and anxiolytics or antianxiety substances: These include phencyclidine ("PCP," "Angel Dust) or similar acting arylcyclohexylamines, which may induce *delirium psychosis*, *catatonic mutism*, *coma*, agitation, confusion, or violence. Benzodiazepines, benzodiazepine-like drugs, barbiturates, and barbiturate-like drugs are included in this classification.

Substance-related disorders can be divided into two groups. The first, substance-use disorder, refers to abuse of the substance. When Tom began to use alcohol routinely to feel at ease with other people and when he began experimenting with alcohol to determine his preferences and the amount needed to achieve the effect he desired, he was exhibiting a substance-use disorder.

Then, when Tom became intoxicated on a regular basis and became dependent on alcohol, he had crossed over into the second group, substance-induced disorders. Substance-induced disorders can cover a range of situations and behaviors, including intoxication and later withdrawal, both of which Tom experienced. Depending on the substance used, substance-induced disorders can also cause *delirium*, *dementia*, amnesia, *psychosis*, mood disorders, anxiety disorders, sleep disorders, and sexual dysfunction.

Most people who are dependent on addictive substances develop an uncontrollable craving for that sub-

When heroin was first produced, it was legal. In fact, the same company manu-
factured it that today sells Bayer Aspirin.

Dual Diagnosis—Drug Addiction and Mental Illness

stance. For example, when Christiane started taking an occasional cigarette out of her mother's purse so that she could join her friends for "a smoke," one cigarette a week was enough, and her mother was none the wiser. A Saturday-afternoon cigarette smoked in a small clearing in the park was all that was necessary for the group of nine-years-olds to feel grown up. After a time, however, the Saturday cigarette was joined by one and then two other cigarettes, which Christiane smoked in her backyard during the week. Over the years, the number of cigarettes she smoked weekly and then daily continued to escalate. She smoked during several bouts of bronchitis, even though her doctor warned her sternly that she was placing her health in serious jeopardy. Her use of cigarettes was the cause of a breakup with her boyfriend.

By the time Christiane reached her third year of college, she was determined to give up her fifteen-cigarettes-per-day habit. But it wasn't easy. Relapses are common when attempting to control or eliminate use of an addictive substance and recover from a substance-related disorder. Christiane tried several methods and went through many disappointing relapses before eventually succeeding. She has now been nicotine free for over a year, but she still fights the occasional temptation to light up a cigarette. Because Christiane has not smoked a cigarette in twelve months, she is considered to be in sustained full *remission*.

With the exceptions of nicotine and caffeine, use of any of the remaining classes of substances listed earlier can result in substance intoxication. The symptoms of intoxication can vary, depending on the substance used. When Tom drank a moderate amount of alcohol he became more relaxed and talkative. But as he consumed ad-

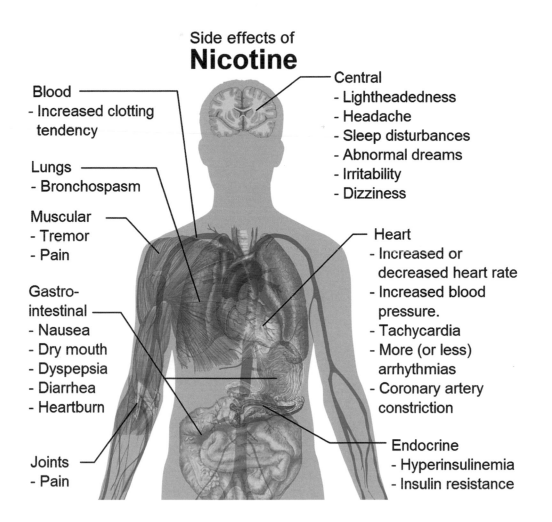

Side effects of
Nicotine

Central
- Lightheadedness
- Headache
- Sleep disturbances
- Abnormal dreams
- Irritability
- Dizziness

Blood
- Increased clotting
  tendency

Lungs
- Bronchospasm

Muscular
- Tremor
- Pain

Gastro-intestinal
- Nausea
- Dry mouth
- Dyspepsia
- Diarrhea
- Heartburn

Joints
- Pain

Heart
- Increased or
  decreased heart rate
- Increased blood
  pressure.
- Tachycardia
- More (or less)
  arrhythmias
- Coronary artery
  constriction

Endocrine
- Hyperinsulinemia
- Insulin resistance

ditional amounts of the substance, his behavior began to change in more negative ways. For example, Tom sometimes lost his balance and spilled his drink, his mood became changeable, and he occasionally acted toward others in a belligerent manner. Even before he drank enough to make himself ill, Tom's thoughts became muddled and his speech was slurred. All of this happened because the alcohol was affecting Tom's *central nervous system*.

People in the medical field can tell when a person has been drinking excessively not only because they can smell alcohol on the person's breath but also because they can measure it in the person's blood and urine. When an alcohol-induced substance-related disorder becomes more serious, doctors can perform tests on a person's liver to help determine how much physical damage the disorder has caused.

Symptoms exhibited by an individual suffering from a substance-related disorder are dependent on the substance being used, but they are also determined by the person's body chemistry, by the amount of substance used, the duration of use, and other factors. The most common symptoms include impaired thinking, judgment, *perception*, and attention. The person may have difficulty staying awake and experience reduced *psychomotor* ability, or he might have so much energy that he is awake and active all night. The behavior a person exhibits toward others will often be far different than it would be if the substance were not being used.

When someone who has been using an addictive substance in large amounts for a prolonged period of time tries to discontinue use of the substance, she can experience substance withdrawal. This happens because the individual's brain chemistry has changed in reaction to the substance. If the substance is then not available to the brain, the body reacts in uncomfortable ways. Withdrawal symptoms are often the opposite of the feelings that are brought on by use of an addictive substance.

For example, alcohol is a sedative that depresses the central nervous system. For a person like Tom, withdrawal symptoms begin to develop as the presence of alcohol diminishes in the central nervous system, thus causing the central nervous system to react in a *hyperactive* manner. Tom's withdrawal symptoms (anxiety, sweating, shaking, and rapid heart rate) ended after a few days. Other residents of the facility Tom attended, however, had more prolonged withdrawal symptoms. For example, Tom's friend Bob still had difficulty sleeping several months after discontinuing his use of alcohol. Some individuals can even suffer seizures and hallucinations during withdrawal from alcohol addiction.

Alcohol-Use Disorders

There are four levels of alcohol misuse, which are classified based on severity. The first level is known as risky use, and it includes binge drinking and other behaviors in which alcohol can become dangerous. In cases of risky alcohol use, people drink enough to become impaired, and they may make poor choices, such as choosing to drink and drive. The next level is problem drinking, which is the point at which drinking begins to interfere with a person's life. Problem drinkers often suffer from lower grades or lower performance at work, and they are at higher risk for long-term alcohol-related health problems. The third level is alcohol abuse, which occurs when a person continues to drink heavily on a regular basis, despite the negative effects that they are experiencing. The most severe alcohol-use disorder is alcohol dependency, or alcoholism. At this stage, the person's body needs alcohol to function. They are addicted, and it is extremely difficult to stop drinking. Stopping cold turkey can lead to serious, sometimes life-threatening withdrawal symptoms, and so alcoholics should only stop drinking under the supervision of trained health care providers.

Main physiological effects of
Crack cocaine

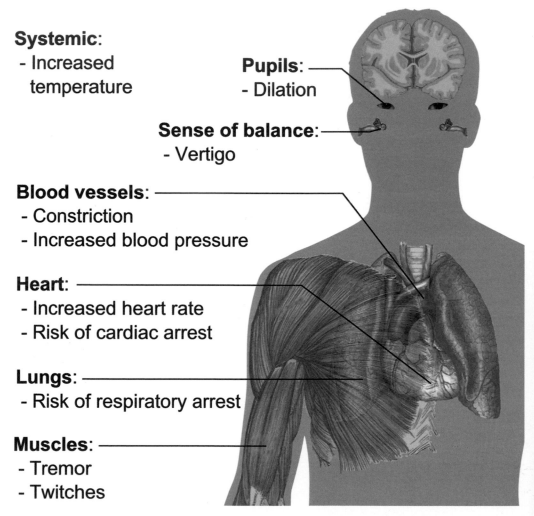

Systemic:
- Increased temperature

Pupils:
- Dilation

Sense of balance:
- Vertigo

Blood vessels:
- Constriction
- Increased blood pressure

Heart:
- Increased heart rate
- Risk of cardiac arrest

Lungs:
- Risk of respiratory arrest

Muscles:
- Tremor
- Twitches

People who successfully conquer withdrawal symptoms and become substance free are said to be in remission. These individuals are extremely **vulnerable** to temptations to use the substance again during the first twelve months following withdrawal, however, and any use of the substance can reinstate the cycle of dependence.

People with active substance-related disorders often experience many health problems. Tanya began experimenting with a wide variety of substances while she was still in high school. Eventually Tanya tried heroin, and it soon became her drug of choice. One of the major health problems Tanya suffered as a result of her dependence on heroin was malnutrition. That's because Tanya's life became totally dedicated to the pursuit and use of heroin. Obtaining the substance and "shooting up" became the only things Tanya lived for. Family and former friends became insignificant to her, and Tanya didn't care about where she lived or slept; she rarely thought about food. All that mattered to Tanya at the height of her substance-induced disorder was obtaining and injecting more heroin. By the time she sought treatment, Tanya had lost a third of her normal body weight and was seriously **anorexic**.

Physical problems brought on by a substance-related disorder vary depending on the substance used and the physical makeup of the person using the substance. For instance, Greg's use of cocaine caused serious erosion of his nasal passages, while Jane's baby was born with a **physiological** dependence on cocaine and had to endure withdrawal symptoms as a result of Jane's use of that substance.

The bottom line is that substance-related disorders are dangerous for many reasons. Illegal drugs are, of course, not monitored by any government agency for purity or for dosage. When individuals use these substances, they may be putting anything into their bodies. Each usage carries with it the possibility of illness from **contaminants** as well as overdose from the illegal substance. Very serious medical conditions such as irregular heartbeat, respiratory distress, human immunodeficiency virus (HIV, the virus connected with AIDS), hepatitis, and bacterial infections from contaminated needles can result from continued use of addictive substances.

A recognizable pattern exists with the repeated use of many addictive substances that helps mental health professionals to diagnose substance dependence:

1. The individual develops tolerance for the substance, meaning that she must ingest more and more of the substance in order to obtain the desired effect.
2. If a person suffering from a substance-related disorder does try to resist the substance, he often experiences a series of unpleasant withdrawal symptoms. These symptoms are usually the opposite of the experiences brought on by the substance. Withdrawal symptoms can lead a person to take more of the substance (or a closely related substance) in order to eliminate the uncomfortable feelings being brought on by withdrawal symptoms.
3. It becomes progressively difficult for the individual to resist consuming the substance, even for one day. In fact, the individual may begin using the substance several times throughout the day. The individual may use the substance for a longer period of time than originally intended and in increasingly larger amounts.

4. The person becomes unable to use a limited amount of the substance even if she has set a limit for herself.
5. Although the individual sincerely wishes to do so, efforts to discontinue use or to decrease the amount of the substance used are unsuccessful.
6. More and more of the person's day may be devoted to the substance (thinking about it, finding ways to acquire it, spending time in areas where it can be used without detection, and actually using it). As a consequence, areas of the person's family and social life might be neglected, as might their employment.
7. Use of the substance continues even if the individual recognizes the negative impact it is having on his well-being, including physical (for example, liver damage caused by alcohol use, malnutrition as a result of heroin use, etc.) as well as psychological problems (for instance, depression following use of cocaine).

Clearly, substance abuse is far more than a bad habit. And it doesn't indicate that a person is "bad" or immoral. Instead, medical professionals believe that substance disorders are truly a form of mental illness.

U.S. Department of Justice Drug Enforcement Administration Drug Scheduling

Schedule I

- The drug or other substance has a high potential for abuse.
- The drug or other substance has no currently accepted medical use in treatment in the United States.
- There is a lack of accepted safety for use of the drug or other substance under medical supervision.
- Some Schedule I substances are ecstasy, heroin, LSD, and marijuana.

Schedule II

- The drug or other substance has a high potential for abuse.
- The drug or other substance has a currently accepted medical use in treatment in the United States or a currently accepted medical use with severe restrictions.
- Abuse of the drug or other substance may lead to severe psychological or physical dependence.
- Schedule II substances include morphine, PCP, cocaine, methadone, and methamphetamine.

Schedule III

- The drug or other substance has a potential for abuse less than the drugs or other substances in Schedules I and II.
- The drug or other substance has a currently accepted medical use in treatment in the United States.

- Abuse of the drug or other substance may lead to moderate or low physical dependence or high psychological dependence.
- Anabolic steroids, codeine, hydrocodone with aspirin or Tylenol, and some barbiturates are Schedule III substances.

Schedule IV

- The drug or other substance has a low potential for abuse relative to the drugs or other substances in Schedule III.
- The drug or other substance has a currently accepted medical use in treatment in the United States.
- Abuse of the drug or other substance may lead to limited physical dependence or psychological dependence relative to the drugs or other substances in Schedule III.
- Included in Schedule IV are Darvon, Talwin, Equanil, Valium, and Xanax.

Schedule V

- The drug or other substance has a low potential for abuse relative to the drugs or other substances in Schedule IV.
- The drug or other substance has a currently accepted medical use in treatment in the United States.

(Source: www.dea.gov)

3 What Is Mental Illness?

People with mental illnesses aren't crazy . . . or nuts . . . or bonkers. Those are slang words that don't mean much in the real world of mental health.

Mental illnesses are medical conditions that interfere with a person's thinking, feeling, mood, ability to relate to others, and daily functioning. Just as asthma is a disorder that interferes with the lungs' ability to do their job normally, mental illnesses are medical conditions that interfere with the brain's ability to do its job. These conditions often result in a diminished capacity for coping with the ordinary demands of life.

Serious mental illnesses include major depression, schizophrenia, bipolar disorder, obsessive-compulsive disorder (OCD), panic disorder, post-traumatic stress disorder (PTSD), and borderline personality disorder. These illnesses can affect persons of any age, race, religion, or income. They're not caused by a person being weak—or bad—or uneducated. They can't be overcome through "will power."

The DSM-IV-TR

When a doctor or psychiatrist decides someone has mental illness, she bases her diagnosis on guidelines from The Diagnostic and Statistical Manual of Mental Disorders, 4th edition, text revision 2000. Better known as the DSM-IV-TR, the American Psychiatric Association publishes the manual and updates it regularly. It covers all mental health disorders for both children and adults, and it also lists known causes of these disorders, *statistics* in terms of gender, age at onset, and prognosis as well as some research concerning the best treatment approaches.

Mental health professionals use this manual when working with people who have psychological problems. The DSM-IV-TR is like the "bible" of the psychiatric world. It uses what is called a "multiaxial" or multidimensional approach to diagnosing because mental illness is seldom caused by just one thing. It's usually a mixture of environmental and genetic causes, for example.

The DSM looks at five dimensions:

- **Axis I: Clinical Syndromes.** These include things like depression, schizophrenia, and *phobias*, anxiety disorders, and eating disorders. Substance abuse disorder is also listed here, as are **ADHD** and *autism*. With the exception of autism, these disorders respond to drug treatment.
- **Axis II: Personality Disorders and Intellectual Disabilities.** Personality disorders are clinical syndromes that have more long-lasting symptoms and encompass the way the individual interacts with the world. They include paranoid, antisocial, and borderline personality disorders. Mental retardation is an intellectual disability.

lenges may make a person more likely to turn to drugs or alcohol as well.

How Common Is Mental Illness?

Experts say that about 6 percent of Americans—about one person out of every seventeen—have a serious mental illness. The National Institute of Mental Health reports that approximately 57.7 million Americans-experience a mental health disorder in a given year, and the U.S. Surgeon General reports that 10 percent of children and adolescents in the United States suffer from serious emotional and mental disorders that cause them significant problems in their day-to-day lives at home, in school, and with peers. According to the World Health Organization (WHO), four of the ten leading causes of disability in the world's developed countries are mental disorders. WHO predicts that by 2020, clinical depression will be the leading cause of disability in the world for women and children.

Depression

Lucy is a twenty-seven year old woman living alone in New York City. Even though she has many friends, she spends most of her time alone at home. She avoids social interaction, and usually only leaves her apartment to go to work. She is sad and lonely most of the time, and it's very hard for her friends to get her out of the house. It's not that she has any problem spending time with them—it's just that she usually doesn't feel like it.

Lucy has a horrible job that she hates going to, but she never feels like there's much of a point to trying to find a new job. He daily schedule is always the same; she wakes up,

Depression is a serious illness.

It is very different from the common experience of feeling miserable or fed up for a short period of time.

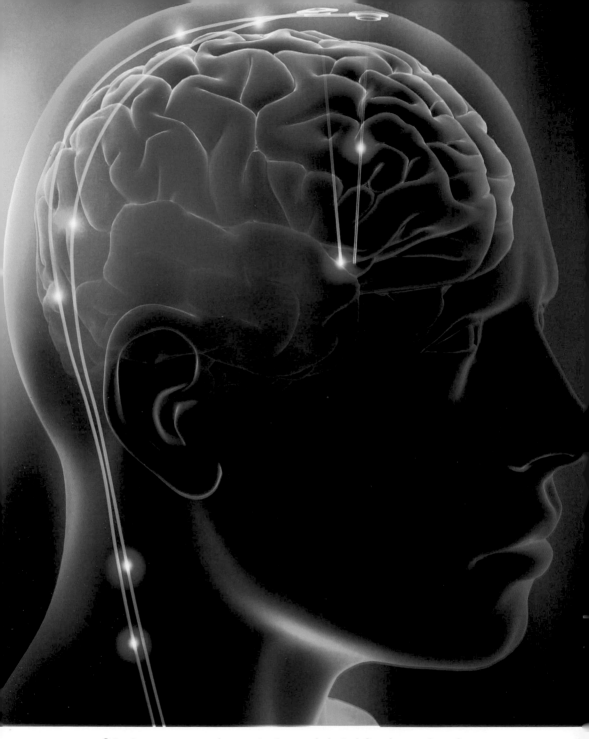

Scientists are more and more viewing psychological disorders, such as depression, as brain disorders, caused by chemicals within the brain not working the way they are meant to.

goes to work, comes home, gets something to eat, and goes to sleep.

She never suspected that she might be depressed. However, she came across an online quiz, which asked her a series of questions about her behavior. At the end, it told her that she may be clinically depressed, and that she should seek help from a health care professional.

Following the advice that she found online, she started seeing a therapist, who diagnosed her with depression. After several weeks of talk therapy and antidepressant medications, Lucy feels much better about herself. She spends less time sleeping, and more time out with her friends and family.

Everyone knows what it feels like to be depressed—sooner or later, everyone gets unhappy and spends a couple days feeling down in the dumps. Clinical depression, however, is a serious disorder where those feelings of sadness just don't go away. When this happens, people feel tired and may sleep a lot less or more than they usually do. They lose interest in things that they used to find enjoyable, and they may begin to gain or lose weight. In serious cases, they can have thoughts of suicide, and may even try to kill themselves.

Depression can have many different causes. One possible cause is genetics, which means that if a person has had family members who have had depression, she is more likely to become depressed, as well. What's going on in a person's life and where he lives can have an effect, as well. Usually a combination of many different factors contributes to the development of a condition like depression.

Anxiety Disorders

Just as depression is when a person can't control his feelings of sadness, an anxiety disorder is when a person can't can't even leave their own house. Other phobias include the fear of being in closed-in spaces, the fear of spiders or other animals, and the fear of blood. When someone has a phobia, she may an intense fear, and she may feel light-headed or have trouble breathing. Sometimes, a phobia can be paired with panic disorder. For example, an agoraphobic person may experience panic attacks when he is in public places.

Schizophrenia

Schizophrenia is a severe disorder in which a person experiences things that are not real, and is often unable to tell whether something is real or not. There are many different kinds of schizophrenia, and people can experience many different kinds of symptoms. For example, some people may see or hear hallucinations, or they may be convinced that the government is trying to kill them. Some schizophrenics can't speak clearly, and others have trouble concentrating or remembering certain things.

There are a few different subtypes of schizophrenia. The first is paranoid schizophrenia, which is characterized by hallucinations and delusions, as well as paranoid behavior, but no other symptoms. Disorganized schizophrenia occurs when a person has disorganized or chaotic thoughts, and sometimes cannot speak clearly or can only speak nonsense. In cases of catatonic schizophrenia, patients are unresponsive and may show random or agitated movement. Finally, undifferentiated schizophrenia is used to describe cases where patients have psychotic symptoms, but don't fit the criteria for the other three types of schizophrenia.

Although the name "schizophrenia" comes from the Greek word "schizein," which means "to split," schizo-

Schizophrenia in the DSM-IV-TR

According to the DSM-IV-TR, a person must display the following symptoms to be classified as schizophrenic:
- Two or more of the following:
  o Delusions
  o Hallucinations
  o Disorganized speech
  o Disorganized behavior, such as dressing inappropriately or crying frequently.
  o Negative symptoms, such as a lack of emotional response, speech, or motivation.
- Trouble functioning in a social or work setting.
- The symptoms must last for a significant time, usually at least six months.

Louis Wain was an artist who was diagnosed with schizophrenia. These paintings of cats were created at different stages of his disease's progression, revealing his increasingly fragmented perception of reality.

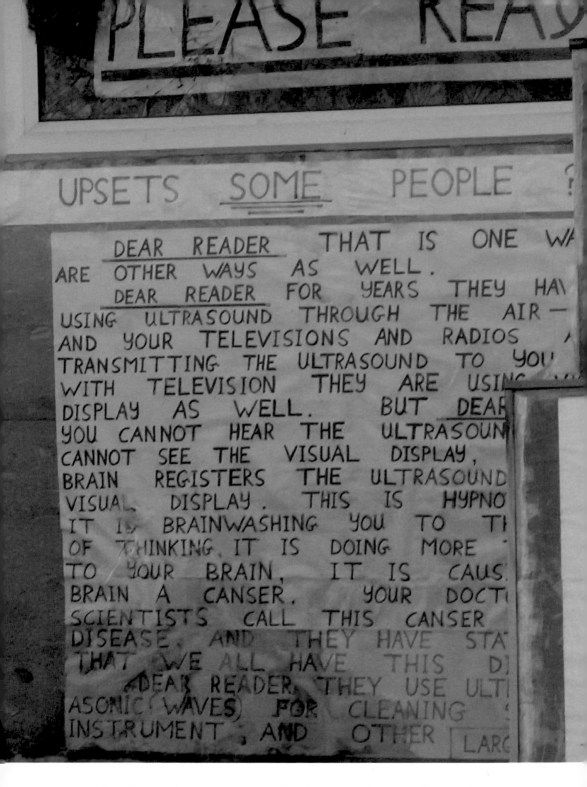

This sign was posted by a person with schizophrenia. It reveals his paranoia and delusions.

Chapter 3—What Is Mental Illness?

Schizophrenia occurs in people all around the world. Darker areas on this map show the regions of the world where schizophrenia is most common, while the light yellow areas show where it is least common. (Data from the World Health Organization.)

phrenia should not be confused with dissociative identity disorder, which is when a person believes that he has more than one awareness inside his head. Instead, schizophrenia is when a mind's ability to function correctly disintegrates. People with schizophrenia may hear voices, and they may believe that these voices have their own distinct personalities, but a schizophrenic patient does not experience the sudden changes in personality and identity that someone with dissociative identity disorder—or "split personality"—does.

No one is sure what the causes of schizophrenia are, but if someone has a family history of mental illness, she is much more likely to be schizophrenic. In addition, where a person lives and what kind of family life he has can have an impact on whether he is likely to become schizophrenic later in life. For most people, symptoms

Many homeless people have untreated mental illnesses. Unable to hold down a job or maintain relationships with others, they have fallen out of society into the streets.

tal illness are more likely to be unemployed. They're more apt to have problems getting along with others and controlling their emotions. They have a greater chance of ending up homeless or in prison. They're more likely to commit suicide. And they're more apt to abuse drugs or become addicted.

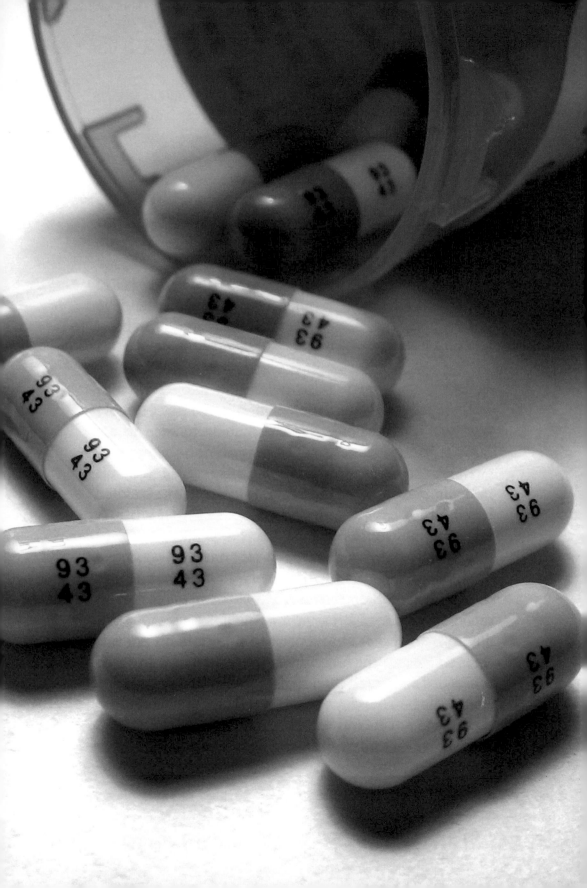

4 Double Trouble

For many people with mental disorders and disabilities, drugs are an important part of life. When someone is simply unable to function due to a serious mental condition, or they have difficulty interacting with people, responsibly used drugs are sometimes the only way to have a normal life. These medications can have benefits like keeping someone's mood swings in check, giving someone a full night's sleep, and helping someone concentrate without getting distracted. Drugs can help control disorders like schizophrenia, obsessive-compulsive disorder, and depression.

Of course, drugs can also have negative effects, if they are used irresponsibly. And recreational and illegal drugs can create a dangerous mix when they're combined with mental disorders. Many people with psychiatric disorders use drugs or alcohol without the supervision of their doctor, to help them deal with negative symptoms of mental conditions or the side effects of other medications.

Of the many people who have an addiction to drugs or alcohol, a significant number also have some form of other psychiatric disorder. When this happens, it is called dual diagnosis: the diagnosis of both an addiction and another psychiatric disorder. Scientists have several theories as to why this double trouble is so common.

Causality Theory

James is constantly afraid that the government is watching him and tracking his movements via satellite, and he has difficulty speaking clearly and getting his point across. Recently, these symptoms have gotten so bad that they have interfered with his life. He has lost his job and he is afraid to leave his house because he thinks the government might be trying to catch him. Luckily, he has a good friend who convinced him to get help from a psychiatrist.

After talking with James for a while, the psychiatrist diagnosed him with paranoid schizophrenia, and prescribed some antipsychotic medication, which helped James control his condition. However, James still had a lot of trouble, and relapsed frequently. His therapist tried him on several different combinations of drugs, none of which seemed to help very much.

After a few more weeks of therapy, James admitted that he had been using marijuana for years, and has been using it more and more heavily recently. His therapist believes the

Researchers have found that marijuana use can be linked to schizophrenia.

Dual Diagnosis—Drug Addiction and Mental Illness 73

The causality theory is says that drug use and mental illness are like a row of dominos tumbling over, one thing triggering another.

two may be connected. In fact, he suspects that James' heavy marijuana use may have actually caused his schizophrenia.

James stopped smoking marijuana after his therapist told him that it might have been related to his schizophrenia. With some more therapy, he managed to get his symptoms under control. He got a new job and is getting support from his family and friends. Thanks to his hard work, he has not had a relapse in almost four years.

The first theory to explain dual diagnosis is known as causality theory. The idea behind this theory is that heavy drug use is what causes mental disorders. This

Heavy marijuana use changes the brain's structure.

Dual Diagnosis—Drug Addiction and Mental Illness 75

theory is supported by the fact that some studies have shown a link between the usage of marijuana and getting certain psychiatric conditions, such as schizophrenia and anxiety disorder, later in life. The exact reason that the two might be connected is unknown, but this has been a popular theory in the past.

How do scientists know that causality theory is valid? Scientists look at the numbers of people who have used a certain drug in the past, and see how likely these people are to develop a mental condition later in life. One study like this one was done by looking at the rates of marijuana use among individuals, and examining the rates at which they developed psychotic mental disorders later in life. It was shown that in most cases, regular users of marijuana were about 40 percent more likely to suffer from psychotic disorders, such as schizophrenia, when they got older. In addition, the heaviest users of marijuana were, in some cases, 200 percent more likely to suffer from such disorders.

The problem with this kind of study is that it cannot say for sure whether it was the marijuana that caused the psychosis later in life, or whether some other factor caused both. What this means is that there could be something that makes a person susceptible to both marijuana use and the development of mental disorders. However, as more and more studies are being done, scientists are beginning to support causality theory more and more.

Another example of causality theory occurs in alcoholics. Often, people who begin abusing alcohol will suffer from withdrawal symptoms when they stop drinking. These symptoms can include the development of an anxiety disorder. It is thought that the overuse of alcohol can alter the brain's chemistry so that when the alcohol is

People who overuse alcohol are more prone to depression and anxiety.

Dual Diagnosis—Drug Addiction and Mental Illness   77

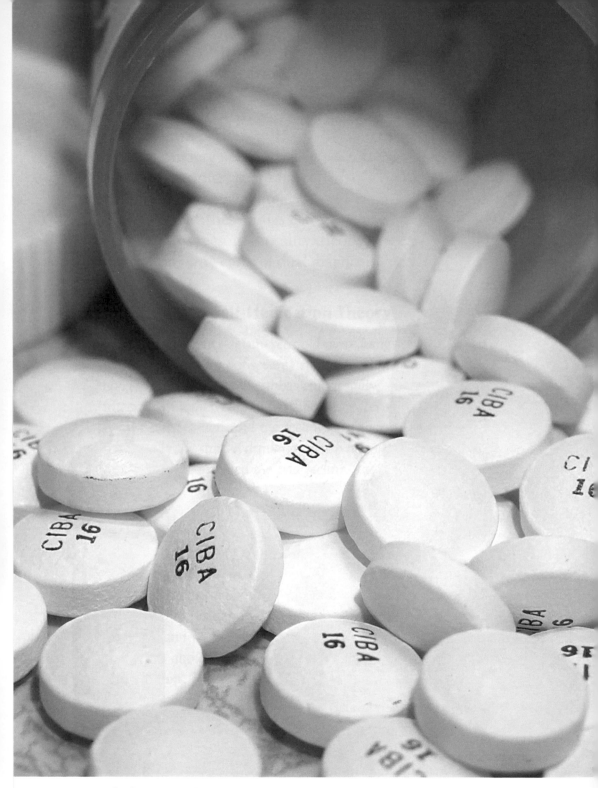

Ritalin is a stimulant used to treat ADHD. People sometimes abuse this drug as a way to make themselves more alert and energetic.

Self-medication theory is the idea that people begin using drugs or alcohol to try to control symptoms from a psychiatric condition that they already have. In addition, some medications for psychological conditions have severe side effects. Sometimes, people will take another drug to make themselves feel better when their medication is causing them distress.

Patients who self-medicate will usually pick drugs with specific effects. For example, some kinds of medication, called depressants, will slow down a people's bodies. People who take this kind of medicine for some other condition sometimes feel like they can't think, or like they're in a fog. To fight this feeling, they may take another type of drug called a stimulant, which will speed them up again. Common examples of stimulants that people use to self-medicate themselves are nicotine, which can be found in cigarettes, or amphetamines, which are sometimes used to treat ADHD.

Another example of self-medication sometimes occurs with patients who are prone to depression or anxiety disorders. Such patients will often self-medicate with alcohol or other depressants such as anti-anxiety medications. Sometimes, a person will become addicted to these drugs, which changes her brain chemistry in such a way that she develops new mental disorders.

One of the problems with self-medication, especially with alcohol or certain antidepressant drugs, is that overuse makes the person's system build up a tolerance to the drugs. As a result, he needs to continually take higher and higher doses of the drug, which can result in serious health concerns. In addition, because he no longer experiences the effects of the drug, the original problem of depression or anxiety actually becomes worse than it was before he started self-medication.

Another problem with self-medication is that normally, a doctor will prescribe a drug to you and tell you exactly how much is safe to take. When people self-medicate, there is no doctor involved and no control on how much they are taking or how often they take it. When this happens, it is very easy for them to become addicted.

The Role of the Amygdala

The brain is not all one unit. It has many different parts, each of which has a specific job to play in our thinking process. We have an area devoted to our sense of sight, an area devoted to making decisions, areas that store our memories, and many others. All in all, the brain is an extremely complicated set of smaller pieces, which work together to create our thought process and keep our bodies running correctly. One part of the brain, which may play a role in dual diagnosis, is the amygdala.

The amygdala is a tiny section of the brain, shaped something like a walnut. It has many jobs within the brain, such as controlling certain emotions. It also stores emotional memories, so when being reminded of something also triggers an emotion, that memory is probably stored in the amygdala. Scientists believe the amygdala plays a role in how we interact with other people, since people with larger amygdalae tend to have more complex social groups. It also determines our decision-making process when we are under stress. One of its most important jobs, however, is controlling our fear response.

Sometimes, it's important to have fear or anxiety. If we weren't afraid, we would constantly be doing things that were dangerous, because we wouldn't be afraid to do

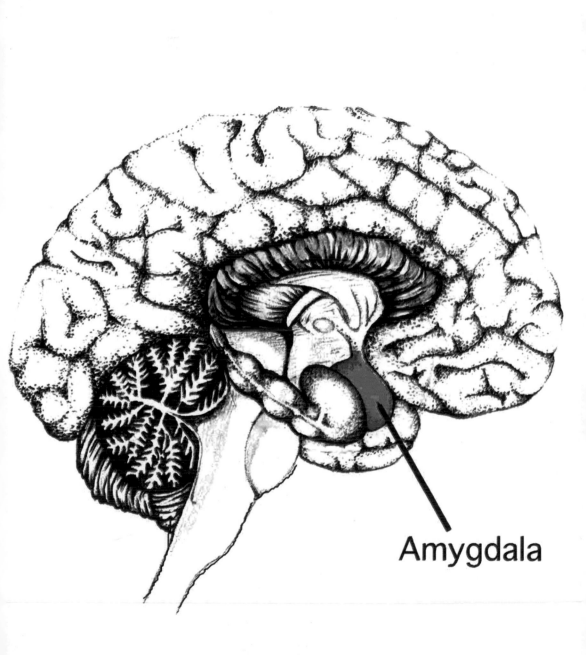

Amygdala

The amygdala is a tiny part of your brain that has powerful effects on your life.

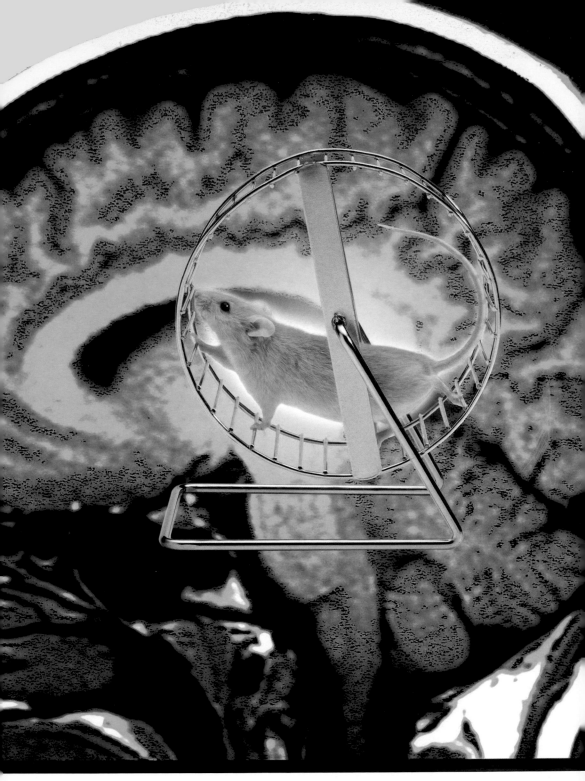

Human brains and rat brains have quite a lot in common. This allows scientists to learn about how human brains function by studying rats.

The Statistics and the Disorders

Up to 50 percent of people with anxiety disorders or depression and as many as 80 percent of people with bipolar disorder, schizophrenia, or antisocial personality disorder also suffer from an addiction to drugs or alcohol. In some cases, a preexisting addiction causes the disorder in the first place. In others, the addiction results from attempts to treat the mental disorder or from self-medication.

Although almost any mental disorder carries with it a higher risk that the patient will also become addicted to drugs or alcohol, there are a few disorders for which this is much more common. These include depression, anxiety disorders, schizophrenia, and personality disorders. These are all Axis I conditions.

them. In addition, being nervous or scared can make us more careful and alert. Sometimes, being afraid is what keeps us alive and healthy.

Sometimes, though, the amygdala doesn't work as well as it should. Scientists tested this in an experiment using rats. One group of rats had a surgery where their amygdalae were damaged, to see if they would behave differently from rats whose amygdalae were left alone. Sure enough, the rats whose amygdalae were damaged showed less fear of new things. They were quicker to explore new areas than the undamaged rats, and they continued playing with the other rats even if the smell of a predator was sprayed nearby. Most important, the rats with the damaged amygdalae were much more sensitive to cocaine than the rats without the damage.

What does this mean for humans? If our amygdalae work in the same way rats' do, then maybe people with unusual or damaged amygdalae are more likely to become addicted to drugs or alcohol. There are a few possible explanations for this. For instance, if a person's amygdalae were damaged, then she would be more adventurous, and more willing to try new things, such as drugs. She would not be as careful about using them responsibly, and so she would be more likely to become addicted.

The role that the amygdala plays in addiction might indicate a reason for the connection to mental disorders. After all, if a person's brain is damaged or incorrectly developed, he will be more likely to have a mental disorder. In particular, irregularities in the amygdala have been connected to the presence of phobias, as well as many other anxiety disorders. Therefore, it could be that some patients have irregular amygdalae, which causes both their mental disorder and their addictive tendencies.

Depression and Substance Abuse

According to the U.S. Department of Health and Human Services, people who have suffered recent episodes of major depression have higher rates of alcoholism and drug addiction compared with the rest of the population. In fact, more than 21 percent of adults who experience serious depression also abuse drugs or alcohol, compared with 8 percent of those not dealing with depression. Young adults who are depressed are just as likely as adults are to turn to drugs or alcohol.

But experts aren't clear which comes first, depression or substance abuse. Depression can cause substance abuse, but substance abuse also can lead to depression. In some cases, both are triggered by some external factor. A person who is going through a rough time because of circumstances in his life may feel depressed—and he may turn to drugs or alcohol to help him deal with the stresses in his life. On the other hand, an addict or alcoholic whose substance abuse problem is out of control can develop depression because of the changes the chemical produces in her brain.

More than a fifth of all adults who are seriously depressed also abuse drugs or alcohol.

Dual Diagnosis—Drug Addiction and Mental Illness 87

How Much Is Too Much?

The National Institute on Alcohol Abuse and Alcoholism has defined "at-risk drinking" as:

- A woman who has more than seven drinks per week or more than three drinks per occasion.
- A man who has more than 14 drinks per week or more than four drinks per occasion.

One drink = one 12-oz bottle of beer (4.5 percent alcohol) or one 5-oz glass of wine (12.9 percent alcohol) or 1.5 oz of 80-proof distilled spirits.

Some researchers believe that individuals with panic disorder, or other psychological illnesses, may have a lower threshold for alcohol tolerance. It may be possible to be "at-risk" even if you are consuming alcohol within the limits described above. If you are concerned about your drinking behaviors, it is important to talk to your doctor or therapist.

seemingly providing relief from anxiety. This is why people with anxiety disorders, including panic disorder and agoraphobia, often use alcohol as a way to cope with fear and anxiety. They are self-medicating in order to reduce their stress and anxiety.

Some researchers have also proposed that genetics may influence both a person's anxiety level and alcohol consumption. These theories suggest that a brain mechanism is responsible for both anxiety symptoms and drinking behaviors.

At any rate, people with anxiety disorders are up to three times more likely to have an alcohol or other substance abuse disorder than those without an anxiety disorder. Studies have shown that problem drinking is more prevalent in certain anxiety disorders, and that typical alcohol use varies between these disorders.

Problem drinking often begins, for example, after the onset of symptoms that go along with social phobia and agoraphobia. For example, someone who has social phobia may fear going to a party where she'll have to talk to people she doesn't know. Just the thought of attending such a gathering produces anxiety. To relax, she self-medicates with alcohol.

Unfortunately, this type of drinking behavior brings big problems along with it. Alcohol consumption becomes a "crutch" the person depends on, so much so that she may avoid social situations where drinking is not possible. Another problem is that long-term alcohol abuse usually builds tolerance to alcohol's effects on the body and brain—and this in turn results in increased alcohol consumption to get the desired result.

Ultimately, what begins as a way to cope with anxiety, can quickly have the opposite effect of increasing distress. Problem drinking leads to alcohol withdrawal—a "hangover." The symptoms of alcohol withdrawal can include:

- anxiety
- panic attacks
- nausea
- vomiting
- elevated blood pressure and heart rate
- agitation
- increased body temperature

These symptoms tend to create a cycle of heightened anxiety and increased problem drinking.

Other drugs can also contribute to anxiety. Chemicals in drugs like cocaine, marijuana, hallucinogens, prescription anti-seizure and pain-relieving medications, and

5 Treatment of Dual Diagnosis

Most mental illnesses, including substance disorders, are treatable. This means that most people who have a dual diagnosis can experience relief from their symptoms by actively participating in an individual treatment plan.

In addition to medication treatment, *psychosocial* treatment such as cognitive behavioral therapy, interpersonal therapy, peer support groups, and other community services can also be components of a treatment plan that assist with recovery.

Getting treated for dual diagnosis is often extremely difficult. Most drug rehab facilities are not designed to accommodate those with severe mental disorders. Similarly, mental hospitals where these disorders are usually treated are not typically equipped to deal with patients who are addicted to drugs. In addition, until recently,

Psychosocial Treatments

Cognitive-behavioral therapy (CBT) is a form of "talk therapy" that focuses on patterns of thinking and the beliefs that underlie such thinking. For example, a person who is depressed may have the belief, "I'm worthless," or a person with a phobia may have the belief, "I am in danger." The therapist encourages the individual to view such beliefs as hypotheses rather than facts and to test out such beliefs by running experiments. Studies of CBT have demonstrated its usefulness for a wide variety of problems, including mood disorders, anxiety disorders, personality disorders, eating disorders, substance abuse disorders, and psychotic disorders.

Interpersonal therapy, which is also a type of talk therapy, focuses on the individual's relationships, with the assumption that mental disorders can be treated by improving communication patterns and how people relate to others. Techniques of interpersonal therapy include identifying emotions, discovering healthy ways to express emotion, and resolving emotional baggage.

Peer support groups are structured meetings of people who share a same problem or psychiatric disorder, usually monitored by a mental-health professional. These groups are opportunities for individuals to give and receive both emotional and practical support as well as to exchange information from people who are going through the same issues that they are.

dual diagnosis was an unappreciated condition. Usually, it was attributed to self-medication. As a result, the traditional approach has been to address the mental disorder, without investigating the drug addiction component as much, in the hopes that it would take care of itself once the psychiatric condition was being properly treated. More recently, however, many treatment plans focus on the substance abuse problem first, with the understanding that a person cannot begin to tackle other problems until he is free of chemical dependence.

Substance Abuse Treatments

Like many individuals who develop a substance-related disorder, Tom spent a certain amount of time in denial before he finally sought treatment. At first, he told himself he only drank at parties. After he started drinking on other occasions, he told himself he was just bored, then just experimenting, and finally just relaxing. *I don't need to drink, I want to drink. I can stop any time, I just don't want to yet.* All these thoughts went through his head—right along with the alcohol that was affecting his brain.

Individuals are not ready for treatment until they recognize that they have a substance-related disorder. Often family members, friends, and medical professionals can help the individual realize that the condition exists and

People with psychiatric disorders often need both counseling and medication to help them overcome their condition.

needs treatment. Once an individual does understand that he has a substance-related disorder, unless he is involved in a crisis situation (such as an overdose of the substance or severe withdrawal symptoms that warrant emergency treatment), it's a good idea to review all of the options for treatment before entering a program.

Some individuals with a substance-related disorder seek treatment either individually or with the support of family and friends. Others are forced into treatment by the courts after being arrested for possession or use of illegal substances. A person's background, motivation, and system of support are all important factors to consider when determining the ideal approach to treatment for that person.

In the past, treatment options for substance-related disorders were limited to "cold turkey"—simply discontinuing use of the substance. But as we understand now, discontinuing use of an addictive substance is no simple matter. In this chapter we'll take a look at how they are administered.

With substance-related disorders, it is important to remember that a treatment option that leads to lasting remission for one person may not work for another. Treatment must be tailored to meet the needs of the individual. A good first step in the treatment of a substance-related disorder is for the individual to obtain a physical examination and a psychiatric assessment. Some psychiatric medications react with other medications, so it is important for the physician to obtain a history that includes all the medications an individual is already taking. A psychiatric assessment is necessary to determine if there may be underlying causes for substance abuse, anxiety or depression for example, which also warrant treatment.

Often a combination of therapies is used in recovery from a substance-related disorder, including behavioral and vocational education, as well as psychiatric medications. Some psychiatric drug treatments can be administered by any physician, including general practitioners, as well as psychiatrists. Other psychiatric medications, such as buprenorphine, can only be prescribed by physicians who have met specific qualifying requirements. These physicians must notify the Secretary of Health and Human Services that they are planning to prescribe this medication to treat an individual with a dependence on opioids. Behavioral therapy is administered by various professionals, including psychiatrists, social workers, and other counselors. Some treatment programs use group therapy sessions that include individuals who are recovering from substance-related disorders.

While residential facilities are prevalent, including therapeutic communities, hospitals, group homes, and halfway houses, most individuals receive nonresidential treatment. Treatment is usually most intensive in the beginning, while the individual is experiencing withdrawal, and immediately thereafter. This can involve inpatient care or an intensive outpatient program. After successfully helping the individual through detoxification and the first few weeks of substance-free living, treatments can be reduced gradually. For some addictive substances, long-term care is needed to maintain remission. Some form of treatment (usually counseling) is often continued for one or two years.

One controversial detoxification method involves the use of *general anesthesia*. With this method (called ultra rapid opioid detox), opiate-blocking medications (such as naltrexone and naloxone) are administered while the vices. When combined with counseling, methadone treatment can be especially successful, but it is very demanding on the individual in treatment. At the beginning of the maintenance program, she must visit a clinic every day in order to obtain her medication. She will be instructed to take the medication in front of workers at the clinic so they can be certain she has actually swallowed the methadone. Once a week, she must submit a urine sample so that it can be tested for the presence of heroin.

Clonidine is sometimes used in treatment programs for opiate addiction. It is often used in combination with sedatives. Since clonidine can lower blood pressure, the doctor should check the patient's blood pressure to be certain that it is not already low prior to treatment with this medication. Sometimes clonidine is administered to block withdrawal symptoms caused by heroin use, and it is usually effective after just a couple of doses. The individual's blood pressure should be recorded each day during this procedure. The dose is usually 0.1 to 0.3 milligrams administered three times each day for five days. After that, the dose is reduced, but treatments are continued for up to two weeks. At this point, physical symptoms of withdrawal should have subsided, but the individual may still have a strong desire to use heroin. Counseling on a long-term basis is often part of the treatment for a substance-related disorder that involves heroin. Methadone may also be prescribed to help the individual resist relapsing. Later in the treatment program, clonidine is sometimes used to help **wean** the individual off methadone.

Buprenorphine is another treatment option for those with a dependence on opioids. The individual's heart rate and breathing must be monitored during withdrawal treatment. It is administered, first as Subutex and then as Suboxone, as a daily tablet placed under the tongue where it is allowed to dissolve. Sixteen milligrams are usually given each day, but some patients respond with as little as twelve milligrams. Then dosage is adjusted up or down as needed to control withdrawal symptoms. Treatment should not be started within four hours of the patient's last opioid use.

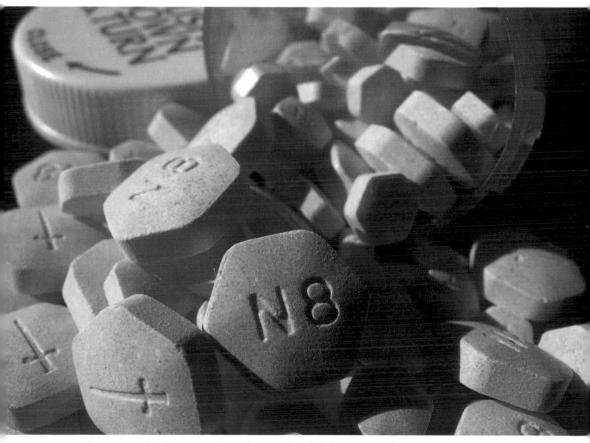

Buprenorphine helps people with a heroin addiction cope with withdrawal symptoms.

your digestive system, blood pressure, and heart rate into turmoil if you dare to ingest alcohol. The individual taking the medication determines the length of treatment. As long as she feels like she needs the extra encouragement it provides to avoid alcohol, she can usually continue use. Some people stay on the medication for years—but anyone who is taking Antabuse should carry a medical identification card. That way, should the patient have an adverse reaction to a product containing alcohol, any medical professionals providing treatment will understand the situation and administer proper care.

Treatment for a substance-related disorder may involve an extended period of time. Many individuals do give in to use of an addictive substance after initial withdrawal and treatment, and some individuals suffer a complete relapse. This does not mean that their situation is hopeless. Instead, it is evidence that their treatment has not been completed and must be extended.

Treatment for Nicotine Addiction

A physical examination is not required before using either nicotine patches or Nicorette gum to aid in conquering an addiction to cigarettes. These products are not recommended for individuals who have unregulated heart disease or for those who are pregnant, however. Withdrawal symptoms experienced when individuals who are addicted to cigarettes stop smoking can include anxiety, impatience and irritability, weight gain, depression, anger, restlessness, and trouble concentrating. Restoring nicotine to the body through the use of patches or gum can block these symptoms.

Nicotine patches are available in several brands and in various strengths. The number of cigarettes an indi-

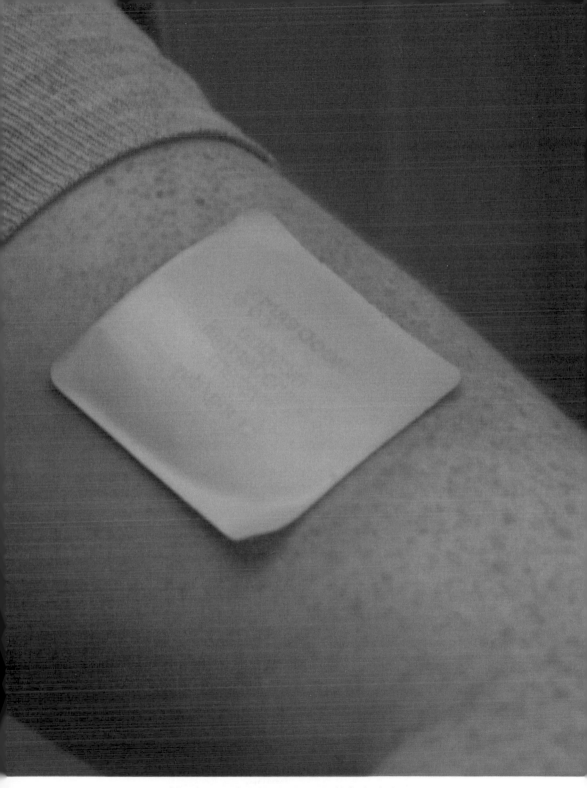

Nicotine patches are one way to kick the habit.

If a person wants to quit smoking, she has several different options, including these lozenges.

vidual usually smokes per day determines the dosage. Similarly, if using nicotine gum to aid cessation of smoking, the number of pieces chewed per day is dependent on the usual number of cigarettes smoked in a twenty-four hour period. Each piece of gum should be chewed slowly for between twenty and thirty minutes, and the number of pieces chewed in a twenty-four hour period should never exceed thirty. Both the patch and the gum immediately begin to deliver nicotine to the body. The majority of available brands of nicotine patches are worn twenty-four hours per day, but one brand is worn for sixteen hours. An individual's craving for cigarettes should begin to diminish with the first application of a patch. As it continues to diminish, patches with reduced nicotine dosage levels should be used. The same thing is true of the gum. A person should use fewer pieces per day as his cravings for cigarettes diminish. It usually takes several months to complete treatment and discontinue use of either the patches or the gum.

People who start smoking before the age of twenty-one usually have the most difficult time conquering the addiction. Some individuals have been treated for this substance-related disorder with the use of bupropion rather than a nicotine product. The bupropion was administered in the form of pills and was taken for seven to twelve weeks.

Because depression is often linked to smoking, antidepressants, such as Prozac, are sometimes part of an individual's treatment. Naltrexone and clonidine have also been utilized in treatment, but thus far, nicotine itself, in the form of patches and gum, remains the major treatment for this substance-related disorder.

SSRIs

Serotonin is a neurotransmitter, one of the chemicals that help your nerve cells communicate with each other. When a person has healthy levels of serotonin, they feel good, and their brain is working normally. Sometimes, though, a person's brain produces too much or not enough serotonin, which can cause a mental disorder, such as anxiety disorders. One of the most common types of drug to treat anxiety disorders is known as an SSRI, or selective serotonin reuptake inhibitor. When a patient who is not producing enough serotonin takes an SSRI, it helps prevent the serotonin that they already have from being reabsorbed, which helps to keep their serotonin levels normal.

MAOIs

Not all cases of a mental disorder respond to the same kinds of drugs. In cases where drugs such as SSRIs and other anti-anxiety medications are not effective, another type of drug, called Monoamine Oxidase Inhibitors, or MAOIs, may be taken. Normally, MAOIs are not prescribed unless all other options have failed because they can be extremely dangerous. When mixed with a chemical called tyramine, which is found in liver, alcoholic beverages, and certain types of cheese, MAOIs can cause dangerous high blood pressure. This can lead to the patient experiencing a stroke or heart attack if it is not treated. In addition, combining MAOIs with a wide variety of other medications can lead to extremely dangerous effects. Normally, a person who is taking MAOIs will carry a card to inform emergency health care providers that they need special consideration when being given food and medications.

warning after a long period of improvement. Since drugs are so unpredictable in their effectiveness against schizophrenia, for example, relapses are particularly common with this disorder. Controlling the symptoms of schizophrenia is an ongoing process throughout a person's life. There is no single drug that can be used to treat schizophrenia, and most people have to try several different drugs before they find one that helps them control their condition. Many of these drugs have severe side effects, however. As a result, it is frustrating for a patient to find the correct drug or combination of drugs that they need to help themselves.

The most important thing for a person with a dual diagnosis is that he gets treated for both his mental disorder and his addiction. This means that an integrated approach is necessary. In other words, treatment should work together to address both problems at the same time. Just as the causes are twined together, so are the answers that will help people cope with a dual diagnosis.

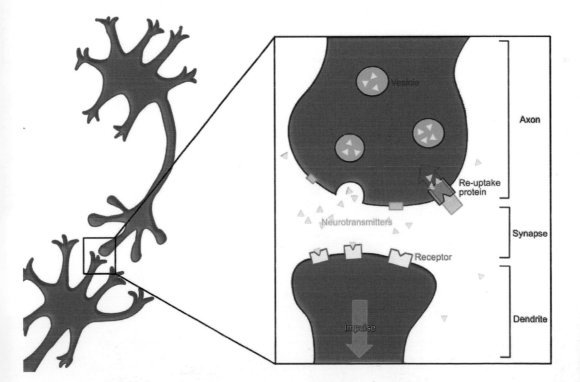

SSRIs work by making sure that there is enough of the neurotransmitter serotonin to carry messages between nerves. This reduces both anxiety and depression.

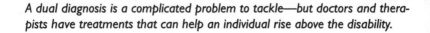

A dual diagnosis is a complicated problem to tackle—but doctors and therapists have treatments that can help an individual rise above the disability.

What Do Rehab Programs Accomplish?

Abstinence

In many cases it seems that as long as the substance is in the blood stream, thinking remains distorted. Often during the first days or weeks of total abstinence, we see a gradual clearing of thinking processes. This is a complex psychological and biological phenomenon, and is one of the elements that inpatient programs are able to provide by making sure the patient is fully detoxified and remains abstinent during his or her stay.

Removal of Denial

In some cases, when someone other than the patient, such as a parent, employer, or other authority, is convinced there is a problem, but the addict is not yet sure, voluntary attendance at a rehab program will provide enough clarification to remove this basic denial. Even those who are convinced they have a problem with substances usually don't admit to themselves or others the full extent of the addiction. Rehab uses group process to identify and help the individual to let go of these expectable forms of denial.

Removal of Isolation

As addictions progress, relationships deteriorate in quality. However, the bonds between fellow recovering people are widely recognized as one of the few forces powerful enough to keep recovery on track. The rehab experience, whether it is inpatient or outpatient involves in-depth sharing in a group setting. This kind of sharing creates strong interpersonal bonds among group members. These bonds help to form a support system that will be powerful enough to sustain the individual during the first months of abstinence.

"Basic Training"

Basic training is a good way to think of the experience of rehab. Soldiers need a rapid course to give them the basic knowledge and skills they will need to fight in a war. Some kinds of learning need to be practiced so well that you can do them without thinking. In addition to the learning, trainees become physically fit, and perhaps most important, form emotional bonds that help keep up morale when the going is hard.

(*Source*: Partnership for a Drug-Free America.)

Picture Credits

American Psychiatric Society: p. 52

Andreus: pp. 26, 58

Balik, Petr: p. 75

Blooplers: p. 94

Cammeraydave: pp. 23, 84

Casey, William: p. 77

Creative Commons: pp. 109, 117

DEA: p. 21

Depression Alliance: p. 57

Electropower: p. 102

Flagstaff Fotos: p. 61

Fruitsmark, Steven: p. 64

GlaxoSmithKline: p. 110

Gunnar3000: p. 74

Harding House Image Creation: p. 97

Haggstrom, Mikael: pp. 41, 44

Jaros, Miroslav: p. 24

Joruba: p. 79

Krishna Creations: p. 8

Lacroix, Alain: p. 67

Marcinski, Piotr: p. 87

MPV-51: p. 39

Mysid: p. 30

NAABT: p. 105

National Academy of Sciences: p. 29

Oneo2: p. 112

Pargeter, Kirsty: p. 118

Pettinati et al: p. 101

Radu, Balint: p. 10

Redock, Barbara: p. 68

Saporob: pp. 13, 18

Skypixel: p. 50

Steidl, James: p. 114

Strock, Michael: p. 66

Thompson, Paul: p. 88

Tromeur, Julian: p. 16

U.S. Fish and Wildlife: p. 73

U.S. Library of Congress: p. 34

Varco, Tom: p. 70

Wain, Louis: p. 63

World Health Organisation: p. 65

Author and Consultant Biographies

Author

Malinda Miller is an author from upstate New York who has written several books for young adults.

Series Consultant

Jack E. Henningfield, Ph.D., is a professor at the Johns Hopkins University School of Medicine, and he is also Vice President for Research and Health Policy at Pinney Associates, a consulting firm in Bethesda, Maryland, that specializes in science policy and regulatory issues concerning public health, medications development, and behavior-focused disease management. Dr. Henningfield has contributed information relating to addiction to numerous reports of the U.S. Surgeon General, the National Academy of Sciences, and the World Health Organization.